Toccata & Fugue

Timothy Kelly

FLOATING
BRIDGE
PRESS

Acknowledgments

Toccata & Fugue is the winner of the 2005 Floating Bridge Press Poetry Chapbook Award.

"Forearm Dissection" is forthcoming in *Field*.
"Toccata" previously appeared in *Nerve*.
"Bent Flashing" is forthcoming in *The Healing Muse*.

Cover designed by Jules Remedios Faye.

The printing of this chapbook was supported, in part, by grants from the Breneman-Jaech Foundation, the City of Seattle Office of Arts & Cultural Affairs, 4Culture, and the Washington State Arts Commission.

Floating Bridge Press
Richard Hugo House
1634 11th Avenue
Seattle, Washington 98122
www.scn.org/arts/floatingbridge

Toccata & Fugue

To my patients and teachers

Love's mysteries in souls do grow
Yet the body is his book . . .

— *John Donne*

CONTENTS

WAKING THE DOZERS

Wherever they are, tripping
and twitching on their morphine drips,
or laid out lax in a dayroom, I squeeze
their feet, sing out their names, fetch them,
Orpheus-like, back to the too-brilliant brim
of the world. There is,

of course, bewilderment. There are lines
and belts and their legs lifted twiglike
and swept out of bed. There are their knees
blocked by my knees, the calibrated
leaning back, and the length of them
levered up to some brief, provisional

perpendicular. Let me see your eyes
I say then, and most, hummingbird-
hearted, do. And we rock a minute
on the linoleum while they reacquaint
themselves with the sheared apart and
strangely wired-back-together world

they've been, for the last while,
out of. It's not fixed yet, they say;
put me back to bed. And I say it is fixed,
really. Let's try some steps.

The Anatomical Position

Stiff, straightarmed, muscular,
nude, palms swiveled forward as if pleading
bafflement or harmlessness halfheartedly,
he called to me from the doctor's wall
as my mother described my flealike dis-

tractability in excruciating detail. A hod
carrier, I thought, a plasterer; a half-
mauled lion tamer staggering, his left side
precisely scored and peeled, his right
utterly unscathed. The barked, maypole leg,
the torn-away face, the muscles twisting
down the length of the arm like a slotted
rapids, stopped. Here, I thought,

was the key, the arcane rigging, elegant
clockworks from which all human
achievement sprung. If I could learn *this*,
I thought; if I could fix it in my head and
call it back whole, layer by excavated layer:
the impulse to forage, to move deeper, to
stumble on the viney cottage deep
in the woods, lit, unguarded; the impulse
to knock; to go in.

WHAT I KNOW

Ida's bled *temporally*, into the bone honeycombing behind her ear,
and, having worked a week with a walker, we're attempting to
cross the soaring, hivelike hospital lobby, and get ourselves out
into the actual, breezy, sun-dotted day. Yesterday, at the Cowlitz,

I imagined this world torn overnight, like some reconsidered
message, in half, unable to move or feel my right side, to speak.
And thought too about the violence visited each day, right as rain,
on the brave peacemakers and blessedly meek. We picked our way

up the bank, my oldest and I, casting around snags and sumps
for steelhead. Maybe, I thought, half the world's *already* withheld
from me, excised, blotted; maybe the half that, glimpsed, compels
the pilgrim, illuminates his path, grants him, in his relentlessness,

peace. This is what I was thinking when a lime-green, ruby-
throated hummingbird paused, wings wide, chest out, throat pulsing,
a foot in front of my face. The air between us thrummed. Cole's line,
like an elegant, looping signature, repeated itself, hissing, overhead.

On Anatomy Being Destiny

We disarticulate our ankle
with a hundred circumferential cuts,
the crosslaced ligaments isolated,
appreciated, incised; the snug, bony
mortise and tenon, with effort, prized

apart. Then I have the foot
in my hand, the gray, rubbery,
horn-nailed thing it will take us two
more weeks to grasp, wondering
down through the springtight rigging,
sleek tendon sheaths, the brilliant,
helical twist-lock puzzle

of its bones. First, though, I walk
the foot to the old lab's window
where the day's dull sky has peached,
and make it jig on the sill, a little
heel-toe my wife taught me
in a bar in Cincinnati in 1979. I
didn't much like her then. Or

the dive with its funky jars
of gristled pigs' feet lined up
at the registers. But she had danced
there to various fiddling for years
on Fridays, in pleated skirt and

stocking feet, and would again that night,
pivoting crisply, passed laughing
hand to hand. I wouldn't dance. So
she asked me to hold her shoe.

Handling Necks

They relinquish their heads
with relief, with dread, as one
relinquishes one's newborn, with
brittle smiles and basketed
hands, to insinuating strangers
who mug and coo. And I, from
behind, make a sling of my fingers,
draw their heads to me, and
with the subtlest oscillations, test.

And much is said, as much is
always said with touch, so that
the name I give what's paining
them, when I help them back to
sitting, shimmers and hangs etched
in the air, like the name of the low
constellation my first summer
lover traced for me as we lay deep
in the dune grass, cooling, me giddy
on nothing but her great, grinning
face and the suddenly swung-open
safe of the sky.
                            Bring poems
to weddings, poems to subways,
poems to the finch the cat's pinned,
twitching. But bring touch to
newborns, touch to the bewildered,

touch, in its calming, discriminating
intelligence, to the ones you've
been given to love. Bring touch
to the place where the speaker's
paused, to prevent him from
launching in again too soon.

TONGUE

Glossals, glottals, linguals, trills,
the organ's hundred stops, mid-fugue, slid out.
Your wagging tars, lashings sting, slips speak
volumes; your clapped-in dance against palate
and teeth sculpts every note of mouth's music.

In the Garden, the stemwinder spoke *sotto voce,*
sibilant, tip-split, seedsowing, slyly inclining Eve;
then the bite, the bright bath of juice, stars and
heavens scintillated; the browsing creatures pause,
barely named; the world, in a swallow, remade.

And now, on a hike in the Hoh, my youngest's
pried loose his last milktooth, a bicuspid, and,
Cleopatra'd on a furry, fluorescent green log,
he holds the white kernel out to me, bloody and
stubbed, on the flat-pink blade of his tongue.

Expressive, receptive, sword, shield, taproot,
drill, flower and leaf, you are praise's plunging
prow, gratitude's dipped oar. But first and last
you are *flesh*, the only muscle the Maker leaves,
at one end of its weave, unattached. Loller,

flicker, mop, flag, there is no God but God, *say it,*
no poem that does not spring from that barbered
bud-bed, resonant, savory, strong. When

the slot slides open, let me make my confession:
I put my tongue to it, father, was that wrong?

I wanted to hear that ascending song.

HEART

1.

Muscles rest, save
one, knock wood,
mine's ejecting nicely.
But mind that
the fearsome shushing
will one day stop

and the murmurs and
orchestral valve clatter,
and the houselights
suddenly dim. And
we'll hold our breath.

2.

Parked one Friday night on Airport Road
under the sensational, starshaking jetpath,
she put my hand on her heart and asked me
to pledge allegiance. And there began
a recurrent dialog on constancy: two stroke,
centripetal, piston shot, bobbin and shuttle,
one ball dribbled constantly 50 years, no
letup, in the same cavernous gym. Even if

you simply sit and acknowledge the wrack
your heaving mind tosses steadily on shore,
each thing luminous, held open patiently, like

a coat; even then, march-cadenced, the heart.
One spring Saturday, we watched the famous,
stumplike, aristocrat Russian sisters beat a rug
in the yard next to my grandmother's with two
tennis racquets, each of them grim-faced,
head-scarfed, grunting and whacking away
in a wooly cloud, from opposite sides, in turn.

BREATH

Flutestem, firefeeder, flue swift;
it ends. It begins again: valve key,
tent flutter, umbrella shot open
in a crowded elevator car. Her ribs,
bound at each end, lift: an inspiration;
the spoke-stiffened rim turning
trimmed, true, around the bearing
and race of the heart. Noble words,
insulting asides, love moans, sorry

singing are cut from the same cloth,
air split off, redirected, forced up
through lapped and tensioned reeds,
resonating in the chambered chest and
head. It pinks the newborn, baffles
the drowning, blasts alien objects
out of the head with a sneeze. And
sitting, in the brief balm of a quiet
mind, there's no silence, no. There's
that old saw —

SURFACE ANATOMY

1. Greater Trochanter

My cupped palm
gripping the knob of her hip
like a shipwrecked man
hauling himself, gasping,
onto rocks. The flared
bowl of the pelvis turns on
an axis running through
that point, and the world, if
you ask me, with it. Rocker,
archangel, indelible signature
written as she strides, silk
dress dancing, past.

2. Spinous Process

Stump farm, goat hop,
streambed, cairn, dish
stack risen from the sink.
Chimneystones, rosary,
salt-rimed archipelago,
ridgebacked crocodile
sunk down cool in mud.
When you unfasten your

bra, my fingertip traces
down the stony draw,

the pan heads, seed beans,
thumbworn horn keys,
abacus beads at the end
of a complex calculation,
judged reasonable, shot back.

3. Patella

Shuttles on a short sash
each time you scissor your knee:
palm-sized, badge-shaped, slick-
backed, it floats
                    and speaks
as sleepers speak, in guttural
grinds and worried whispers
when loaded and forced
to move. Biscuit-top, trivet,
lozenge, soap-stub,
                        we check
its ride, seating, squint and tilt.
It's mashed a thousand times
a day against the femur's face,
to straighten and step, snap off
a leap, stand you startled,
unclasping, from a chair.

AN X-RAY OF A FOOT

In some sealed, smudgy, smokehouse
world, the spray of bones dangles, etched
and weathered, pouring out light. Here
are two dozen irreducible truths puzzled
together, the mortise, tenon, splines and
splices that conform uncomplainingly,
step after step, to a relentlessly irregular
world; that stiffen, twisting, to lever you
reciprocating, mind miles away,

forward. From that slender pivot, the rest
of the scaffold rises, vertical, crossbrace,
straight bone by flare, elegant architecture
engineered to bear weight, bear flesh,
bear stops, spins, violent redirections, and
slow passages of serendipitous, sanctifying
grace. And isn't that, finally, the point?
Your nose brought thoughtlessly down to
the dizzying, pink-dotted daphne, the violet
of the swallow's plunge, the hard things
at the center of each lasting story, luminous,
resonating, strangely articulated, true.

EXPOSITION

In the slow-drifted, dialing-down day, when
swallows, in legion, crowd onto the high
tension lines above Route 10 and kibitz, buzzed
like machinists at the *Pearl* payday afternoons,
singing out in their blue union shopcoats,

I'm listening to my scripture-citing neighbor
Ray tell me the story of the all-midget porn
flick he watched last weekend at an epic
three-day bachelor party that ended in a Portland
suburb with a County Sheriff lightshow and

cruiser convocation, and a dog who looked
like Edward G. Robinson ralphing chunks
of Chinese carryout onto his shoes at three a.m.
It's an embroidered story, very like the ones
the new quads and paras try out on staff

a month into rehab, when their girlfriends
have bailed and they slyly produce photos
of their pretzel-bent cars at the wreckers'. In
that moment, they say, everything flies past
slo-mo: gravel, stopsign, the pinwheeling, tree-

barking 360, and the consequent transected
cord. Once it was all about dayjobs, backrent,
bitch bosses, the chronically-wasted paycheck

to paycheck scuffle. Now, chairbound,
circumspect, they reappraise. It wasn't so

bad, they say. In fact, it was fucking, all
told, great. They want to go back to that last
pint and pipeful, that pivotal, slipped-traction
moment. That flown life; that hard, bitter
thing they hated; *that*. They want that back.

NOTES FROM A PHYSICAL THERAPY CONFERENCE

In the frigid, fluorescent cadaver lab, fume-addled dissectors
are trying to fathom how the body's two hundred bones can
flow so seamlessly around an axis, refined continuously from

one fluid constellation to the next. Yesterday, for instance,
we took apart the act of throwing: a boy blasting lead-bottomed
milk bottles at a fair; or the bowie knife that pins the squirrel

quivering to a tree. There, every joint in skeleton's chain's
recruited, instantaneously drawn to task. It's an old program:
legs set, trunk coiled, arm whipped, and missile intersecting

the tracked object remotely, with consequence. I want to
be the one who recites to you the litany of linked levers that
lets a dancer, perfect line, serenely balance on a toe. I want to

grasp the pelvis. I want to be the one who sees the angles
and graphs the curves, the electrified engineer who can't stop
pointing out where, when she moves, she moves from.

VOLUPTUOSITY

The body's curving comes
to the hand like the dry fields
rise to rain, like risen bread
rounds off in heat, like a pie,
baking, rises to the attic must
of your grandmother's house
where you and your cousins,
winter Sundays, pawed up and
pored over treasure. Like a well-
made tool, the palmed body
docks and snugs, convex to
concave, with heft centered
and a contouring, wraparound
grip. Nothing, not even the long
bones, are truly straight; every
line bowed, every end flared,

cupped, clubbed, and I say
thank God, since most hold
we're made in His image, and
I can hook your hair behind
your ear and study the swirled,
cartilaginous flower I funnel
these driftboat lullabyes into,
tracing distractedly your hip
rounded high in sidelying, incline,
decline, and watching night rise

nest to nest, branch to branch,
muting talk, slowly sealing
the day's high cylinder with its
ball-domed, birdshot, light-riddled lid.

MEDITATION ON ANATOMICAL VARIATION WHILE CHAPERONING MY YOUNGEST SON'S CLASS OUTING TO A CHRISTMAS TREE FARM

The plantation firs stretch densely in all directions,
a uniform, sculpted sea the kids are given leave to
weave through while the adults, craning on tiptoe,

peer, unpenetrating, over. In the distance, gargling
chainsaws rise in quick flights of twos or threes, and
shriek operatically, like clouds of wasps, warring. It's

the crews of convicts, we're told, barbering the trees
conical. Yesterday, at work, a new, boot-top amputee
complained, irony-free, about the dearth of unattached

men as we practiced doing stairs in the dank stairwell
without crutches. And though she was beautiful, I would
never in a million years say those words to a patient,

though it's been more than once the one thing I felt
I really *ought to* have said. And the not-saying pricked
me all morning, until I could corral it, over lunch,

into the gated livestock pen where my lifetime of
Never Said Things are kept. They tunnel out at night,
of course, and disfigure you with sharp tools, though

it's the kind of damage only exes can, in retrospect,

see. Meanwhile, new lovers wander around in warm,
honeycombed suspensions, working to forestall the day

when the tics, asymmetries and deep structural damage
finally register, and you see them for the monsters that
you had somehow, until that point, failed to grasp they are.

Forearm Dissection

The fine, sheathed muscles laid in length-
wise, lapped, lank, orderly as slatted blinds
or a furrowed field, their far ends tapered
to ribbon to glide shiny through the wrist's
cinch, then bending from the bottleneck
in an well-ordered sort, a fine-gauge,
pegged-tight coursing to predetermined
anchorage at the phalanx of a finger.

I'm thinking of a section of saxophonists
in an Ives concerto, in a passage where
birds lift from trees, not playing but
drumming their horn-keys ten, fifteen seconds
with their fingers, so that the clatter, if you
close your eyes, becomes the rising din
of beating wings. Am I remembering
that correctly? Music, heavenly,

from profane hand and hollow horn,
bodies curved congruous, accommodating,
each patterned movement, each set
of stops completing circuits, parsing
breath into notes; clipped, voluptuous,
quartered, counted, until the hooded heart
stirs in its basket and rises, jewel-eyed,
intoxicated, wholly colonized, and sways.

BENT FLASHING

This old trouper, longtime no-code, dwindling,
piebald and barely breathing, won't — deepest
mystery — let go. And though he no longer
registers touch, we come in twice a day and range
his limbs, working distal to proximal, small joints
to large, from the colder planets inward toward
the sun, each of the cobbled paths curving onto
a courtyard, someone pacing there unhurriedly
around the single, shimmering bougainvillea,
pulsing red. Yesterday morning, circling

his wrist, I watched a roofer across Yesler
toss long scraps of galvanized flashing down
three stories to an open dumpster, Zeus smiting
staggered Typhos with tetanic, bright-tined bolts.
And later, during my afternoon visit, someone's
sub, stuck below at a stoplight, rattled every
piece of glass in the East Wing's sashes. I was

flexing his forefoot. I paused then, letting
the pulse thrum through me, then turned my hand
and searched the papery curve of his arch
for his. It was thready but there, distinctive
as a signature, an eye's iris, the finger-pad's
whorls we press questioning, answering, into
the hundred mute mysteries of the day.

Toccata

— from the Italian toccare, *to touch. A composition for a keyboard instrument intended to exhibit the touch and technique of the performer, and having the air of improvisation.*

Leave alone the mechanics, the fluid algorithm of swivels
and pivots, the racked joints, small reciprocations, cast arm
feathering, tension measured, trajectory trimmed, to bring
the tip of my finger to the line of your back, then down it
slowly, to the small.

　　　　　　　　　　Twenty years ago, negotiating that curve
for the first time, I'd deciphered, by night's end, the floors
of the mansion, placement of guards, the thwarts and bottle-
necks, the scars' crimped script, the righteous path, the falloff
to thistles, the clearly marked, yellow-flashing *proceed with
caution, yes.*

　　　　　　　　Now, October, the boys and I have loosened
a row of russets with a fork, and are down, elbow-deep in dirt,
feeling for the satin jackets, dragging out the disinterred
with shouts. And later, in a galvanized tub, we scrub them
clean by feel, working over the submerged nubs and ridges
blindly, each finger-pad a transducer, portal, taking in, paying
out, restoring the irregulars, in a muddy roil, their deep,
otherworldly pink.

　　　　　　　　For one moment, the boys move through
the world with a tenderness, an easy grace, and it's a dream,
I think, an improbability, an anomalous, short-lived statistical
trend. And you and I fall into bed each night exhausted, alarms
armed, and turn, in bewilderment, to each other. Some brave
finger describes an arc, a brushed *kanji* character, a slow
downward scrolling of the bleak middle text, a Braille search
for that slender passage where we last, in some previous life,
transported and exclaiming loudly together, left off.

POSITION SENSE: THE 3-D BODY AS HOLOGRAPHIC CEREBELLAR CONSTRUCT

By a thousand miracles subcortically elided,
I've made it down to the perfumed bed
of West Clear Creek, AZ mid-May and am
seated on a great veined boulder midstream
at the hour that the swallows, as if

by prearrangement, force their heads
out of the high holes freckling the slanted,
sidelit sandstone cliffs, and commence
their scissoring, dinnertime, streamtop
arabesques. At my feet, *mimula,* larkspur,

and neat, barbered tufts of native grass,
each blade wiry, blue-spined, nodding
determinedly in the breeze. There is so much
I want in this life that I oughtn't, so much
that takes me wandering, broadcast,

away. Let me slip down to water; let me
balance, plunge; let me be simplified,
baptized, wakened wholly, to the bone,
by the cold. Let me work like the trout
works, minimally, staying deep in shade,

rising to one cue, the current pricked,
the skimming swarm of gnats the swerving
swallows shear through.

What It Is What It Is

Balking body, bag of bones,
hank of hair, tub of guts,
tenement, firmament, sweatshop
temple,

slab of gristle, jar of clay,
bog of primordial soups; drum,
bellows, warren, wormwood, ticking
bomb,

bellows, nutcase, bladder, coil,
bundle of nerves, pound of tongue,
vehicle, vector, medium,
suit,

baggage, bone-loom, Cornell
box, garden climax, bloody show,
mutineer, shark-bait, illusion,
hive,

seedpod, godhead, current
incarnation, satellite, motherboard,
prick, cunt, it, not it, text, slate,
chaff.

The Way In Is the Way Out

The head floats
gyroscopically over
the roll-rimmed, pail-
shaped pelvis; toes
splay, knees piston,
and the cylindrical
trunk, like a Jupiter
rocket, tips forward,

walks the mined
world provisionally,
combing for a soul.
By some odd,
incontestable
miracle, damaged
people heal. This
is the fundamental
message driven
home to me history
by untangled history:

there's no end
to things that oughtn't
happen happening.
The fit crump.
The papery rise
and pink. There's
a pulse and a finger-

pad clocks it;
there's gratitude,
that bone-thin
song stuck sideways
in my throat.

Timothy Kelly was born and educated in northern Ohio, received his MFA from Boston University, and his MPT (Physical Therapy) degree from the University of Washington. His first book, *Articulation*, was published by Lynx House Press, 1993, and his second, *Stronger*, won the *Field* Prize and was published by Oberlin College Press in 2000. His poems, which reflect an abiding interest in the movement, structure, and beauty of the human body, have appeared in *The Iowa Review*, *Crab Creek Review*, *DoubleTake*, and other journals. He works in Olympia, Washington as a physical therapist, teaches periodically at the Evergreen State College, is married and the father of two teenage boys. He spends his spare time swimming, gardening, doing yoga and the laundry, and arguing about whose turn it is to mow the lawn.

This chapbook was designed in Adobe PageMaker and offset-printed in an edition of 500 on acid-free recycled paper. The text typeface is Adobe Garamond. Each cover was letter-press printed by Jules Remedios Faye.

This is number 384 of 500.